#HOWTWOLIVE

We've included hashtags at the beginning
of each chapter; use these to share your
creations with us – we will repost as many
of them as we can!

Instagram @howtwolive
Twitter @howtwolive_
Facebook howtwolive
Snapchat howtwolive
Tumblr howtwolive

CONTENTS

INTRODUCTION

We see the world in rainbows, and How Two Live is our colourful way of life. It's about expressing your inner greatness, owning it and kicking arse. Through this book we invite you to join us on our journey, and step into a world of rad bad awesomeness.

As sisters, and best friends, we're always on the hunt for fun new things we can do together – whether it's whipping up delicious desserts or Sunday night mani-pedis. We've compiled a collection of our favourite projects we hope will keep you and your besties busy, and have included some of our secrets on fashion and blogging too.

We've also included a 'How Two Make an Impact' section in each category, offering tips on how you can use these projects to make a difference to someone else's life, while having a great time. We've been blessed with the kindest mother on Earth, who has always taught us to appreciate, think of others and give back. We want to pass this on by encouraging girls everywhere to incorporate giving into their daily lives.

We hope this book keeps you from ever being bored and inspires you to dream big … and if it leaves you wanting more, please come visit us at howtwolive.com.

Jess and Stef xx

DIY!

SHARE YOUR CRAFTY PICS WITH US:

#howtwolive #howtwodiy

MAKE POMPOM EARRINGS

There are few things in life we find cuter than pompoms – and you can't exactly wear puppies on your ears. Get your daily fix of pompoms by turning them into earrings and make your ears your biggest cheerleaders!

You will need:
- embroidery thread
- needle
- pompoms
- 2 fishhook earrings

Both the thread and earrings can be found at a fabric store. You can buy the pompoms from an online marketplace like Etsy, or if you're feeling like a superstar, why not make your own from scratch? A quick online search will reveal tons of straightforward pompom-making tutorials.

STEP 1

Tie a knot at one end of the thread. Pull the end of thread you haven't knotted through a needle. Push the needle through the centre of the first pompom.

STEP 2

The knotted end of the thread will catch in the pompom. Continue on and pull the thread through the earring loop and circle the thread through the loop a few times to attach the pompom to the earring, leaving 4–5 centimetres of thread between pompom and earring loop, depending on how long you want the pompoms to dangle.

STEP 3

Finish up by tying the thread in a knot through the earring loop. Make sure you double- or triple-knot the thread to keep your pompom in place.

WARNING
Pompoms are addictive and may lead to excessive amounts of fun.

TRICK
If you don't have pierced ears, you can use clip-on-earring backs.

WE LOVE
Our friend and blogger babe Helena from bellsfashion.blogspot.co.uk, who really knows how to rock pompom earrings! (That's her on the left in the photo.)

CUSTOMISE YOUR PHONE CASE

No outfit is truly complete without the addition of a fab phone case, and who needs to fork out the cash for one when they're so easy to customise at home? Grab an old case from the back of your drawer and plan a phoneover afternoon with your bestie!

You will need:
- a bunch of trinkets
- an old phone case
- a hot-glue gun or superglue
- diamantés

STEP 1

Start by gathering anything you'd like to stick on your phone case. Think little toys, rubbers, 3D stickers, plastic flowers and bows … anything with a surface that's flat enough to be glued down.

STEP 2

Use a hot-glue gun or superglue to stick the items to your case – both types of glue can be found at craft stores. Begin by sticking the larger objects on and then add in the smaller pieces.

STEP 3

Fill in the gaps using the diamantés, ensuring every inch of the case is covered.

TIPS

Get the Japanese-style whipped-cream look by using a silicone sealant. You can find this at any hardware store.

It's easy to find cute trinkets online – try sophieandtoffee.com or rockinresin.com.

WE LOVE

Adding an extra level of awesome by keeping everything we stick on in the same colour or theme.

CREATE A FLUFFY CLUTCH

They say you only have one chance to make a good first impression, so make yours one to remember. If the vibe you're wanting to give off is 'I'm a whole bag of fun', the faux-fur clutch is your new BFF.

You will need:
- an old clutch bag
- fake fur
- a hot-glue gun
- needle and thread (optional)
- a zip (optional)

There are two ways you can bring your furry friend to life; the quickest is to punk out a pre-existing clutch by gluing faux fur onto both sides with a hot-glue gun.

Alternatively, if you're feeling extra crafty, start from scratch by sewing two pieces of fur together with the fluffy parts facing inwards. Then turn the material inside out so that the fur is on the outside and stitching on the inside. Attach a zip and you're ready to hit the town.

TIP
If you're using a pre-existing clutch, we suggest using longer-haired faux fur so that all the material edges and glue lines are hidden.

NEXT LEVEL
Opt for a two-tone clutch by using different coloured fur for the front and back.

WHAT COLOUR SHOULD YOUR CLUTCH BE?
- black or white = evenings and formal events
- purple or orange = everyday wear
- two colours = parties

FLORIFY YOUR SHOES

Finding you're a little tired of what your shoe cupboard has to offer? Adding some flower power to your feet is the perfect way to update your too-old-to-wear but too-cute-to-throw-out kicks. Think it's time to get the girls together for a weekend crafternoon!

You will need:
- a pair of plain shoes
- artificial flowers
- scissors
- a hot-glue gun

TIP
You can apply the same steps to florify anything from handbags to headwear.

TRICK
Use loose petals to fill in any gaps, and don't be afraid to pile them on to create texture.

NEXT LEVEL
If you want to take the crazy up a step, opt for flowers in lots of different colours and sizes.

STEP 1
Select a plain pair of shoes. This can be a good time to sort through your wardrobe and breathe new life into some old faves!

STEP 2
Pick up a bunch of artificial flowers in your colour of choice from a craft store. Cut the flowers off the stems directly below the heads.

STEP 3
Use your hot-glue gun to apply glue to the flower petals, then stick them down flat against the shoes.

STEP 4
Repeat this all over the shoes, ensuring you avoid any buckles or loops.

BONUS!

QUICK & EASY WARDROBE REVAMPS

- Bejewel your headphones
- Cut the shoulders out of an old jumper
- Cover your camera strap in fun material
- Transform an old watch by replacing the watchband with fabric

- Convert an old plain tee into a slogan tee with a permanent marker
- Doodle on white sneakers
- Add studs (or a cracked CD broken into pieces) to the collar of an old shirt
- Turn a cap into a visor by cutting off the top
- Tie-dye old white bed sheets
- Wear a short necklace as a headpiece
- Use old earring studs as pins on your pin board
- Cut an old pair of jeans into shorts

HOW TWO
MAKE AN IMPACT!
WHEN GETTING CRAFTY

When you're getting crafty, double up on supplies and use them to put together a few extra pieces, then donate these to a women's centre as Christmas presents. Why not write cards to go with them too?

STYLE

SHARE YOUR STYLISH SHOTS WITH US:

#howtwolive #howtwostyle

WEAR PRINTS FOUR WAYS

Whether you like to flash a cheeky peek of print, or prefer to go all out in hat to heels, we've got a way you can incorporate HTL's answer to basics into any outfit.

STYLE 1

Matching your nails to a print in your outfit is the perfect place to start your love affair with prints and make a bold statement.

STYLE 2

Wearing two pieces in the same print involves minimal styling effort but makes a big impact.

STYLE 3

If you love the clashing-prints look but are a little hesitant to dive straight in, try starting with different prints in the same colour.

STYLE 4

Once you're a print pro, it's time to just go for it! Clash away with mismatched prints all over your clothing and accessories.

TIP
Never utter the words 'I can't pull this off'. Pulling an outfit off is all about having the confidence to do so, and the second you doubt yourself it's all over.

STYLE 1

STYLE 2

STYLE 3

STYLE 4

STYLE-OFF: JEREMY SCOTT VS LAZY OAF

The verdict: Lazy Oaf wins. While we go gaga for designer Jeremy Scott's flawless prints, they tend to be a little out of our price range. UK label Lazy Oaf is our top pick for wacktastic pieces that won't break the bank.

HOW TWO

FIND OUTFIT INSPO

Finding outfit inspiration can happen anytime, anywhere, but sometimes you need to put a little time aside to check out what's trending to stay ahead of the game.

STEP 1

Check out websites like style.com and wgsn.com on the regular, looking out for colours, fabrics and silhouettes that will be taking off over the next few seasons. The pieces you see on the runways won't be translated into mainstream stores for six to 12 months, so use your internet skills to find similar items and become a trendsetter.

STEP 2

Head to a directory site like bloglovin.com, where you'll find an amazing array of street-style blogs that are bound to get your fashion juices flowing. Look for blogs that use affiliate links, so you'll be able to click straight through to buy similar pieces.

STEP 3

Whenever you come across a style soulmate, remember to hit the follow button, so you can check out their page any time you need a hit of inspo. A lot of our favourite brand discoveries have happened via social media; people often tag the brands they're wearing, so make sure you check out who your style icons are tagging, as well as which brands they're following.

STEP 4

Celebrities are lucky enough to have amazing stylists who make sure their celeb clients are always dressed to perfection. Decide which celebs routinely give you outfit envy, and look to them for regular outfit inspo.

DON'T FORGET

Head out into the real world too. Grab a coffee and a park bench, and be inspired by what people in your city are wearing.

TIP

Make sure to pass on the stylespiration to your followers by tagging the brands that you're wearing.

We're always posting on Instagram about cool brands we find, so check out @howtwolive to unearth some gems!

PUT TOGETHER YOUR OWN

LOOKBOOK

Who hasn't fantasised about having a mix-and-match wardrobe like Cher in Clueless to help them get dressed in the morning? While our version is a little less high-tech, we're excited to let you Bettys know that our lookbook tips will help make this dream a reality.

STEP 1

Pull six to 10 items from your wardrobe that you absolutely love. Use these items as a base to create different outfits, mixing and matching them with various other pieces from your closet.

STEP 2

Each time you style a new outfit, take a head-to-toe selfie in the mirror. Make sure you're putting together outfits for several different occasions, so that when you put your book together you'll be able to sort the pics into categories like parties, work, brunch, etc.

STEP 3

Put the pics into a folder on your computer, or print the photos out and put them together in a scrapbook, making sure you create different sub-folders or tabs so you can easily navigate your way around the sections. Next time you need to dress to impress, you can quickly look through your images and select the perfect ensemble!

DON'T FORGET
Accessories can make or break any outfit, so be sure to include them when styling your looks.

GO DIGITAL
Use an app like Closet+ to store and arrange your lookbook images, or create your dream wardrobe with a website like polyvore.com.

TIP
Update your lookbook every six months when you update your wardrobe for the new season.

GET SNAPPED BY A
STREET STYLE PHOTOGRAPHER

Okay, so the paparazzi aren't exactly waiting outside your door, but just because you're not RiRi doesn't mean you can't rock it in front of the cameras! If you're heading out, here are our tips on how to get the photographers to snap you amongst a sea of fellow fashionistas.

STEP 1

Look up what the current season's trends are, and try to incorporate one of these into your outfit, putting your own spin on it. Blogs and magazines tend to feature groups of pics based on what's trending.

STEP 2

Combine the current trend with your fave OTT outfit, complete with killer shoes, bag, sunglasses … the works. Your outfit should be OTT enough to get you noticed, but not so out there that you feel uncomfortable. The key is to rock up with absolute confidence and the photographers will flock to you.

STEP 3

Make sure you've got cards handy with your @s and #s, so photographers can tag you in any photos they post.

WARNING
When you unleash your individual style you're bound to get some backlash, as we know all too well. Don't let it get you down: haters gonna hate!

TIP
Events that usually attract photographers include fashion shows, store openings, markets and festivals.

TRICK
Rock up 15 minutes early to get snapped, as photographers tend to disappear once an event starts.

BONUS!

1. What's your go-to pair of shoes?
a) Sneakers
b) Heels
c) Sandals

2. What fashion statement do you hate?
a) Skinny jeans
b) Gym gear
c) Birkenstocks

3. What's your favourite accessory?
a) Sunglasses
b) Handbag
c) Phone case

4. What do you love getting dressed for?
a) Brunch
b) Wedding
c) Festival

5. Which city would you love to live in?
a) Sydney
b) Paris
c) London

Mostly As: Chillville
You're all about looking cool without having to compromise on comfort. You realise it's all in the attitude and you've got plenty of it (plus a killer sneaker collection).

Mostly Bs: Sharp & Chic
You are the queen of all things pretty. Whether it's taking the dog for a walk or hanging out with friends, you always make sure you bring your fashion A-game.

Mostly Cs: Queen of Quirk
Your style is a little off the beaten track. You're not afraid to bump up the fashion bar and rock up to a party in something that will get people talking.

MAKE AN IMPACT!

WITH YOUR KILLER WARDROBE

When it comes time for your seasonal wardrobe cull, hand over anything you're not wearing anymore to a local op shop. Encourage the rest of your house to do the same, and you can drop off everyone's items together. Better yet, why not host a stall at a market to sell your excess clothing, then give the profits to a charity of your choice? Have fun and raise funds at the same time!

RECIPES

SHARE YOUR DELISH CREATIONS WITH US:

#howtwolive #howtwocook

DISH UP PARTY POPCORN

Ever heard of the saying 'there's a party in my mouth, and everyone's invited'? We're pretty sure that whoever invented this expression said it with a mouth full of party popcorn. This is the ultimate snack and brings all the goods: popcorn, nuts, chocolate (check, check and double-check). We guarantee our recipe will put you at the top of every guest list.

You will need:
- 1 block white chocolate
- 1 block milk chocolate
- 1 bag caramel popcorn
- ½ cup cashews, salted
- 1 cup mini marshmallows

STEP 1

Begin by melting the chocolate in the microwave. Keep the blocks in separate bowls so the white chocolate doesn't mix with the milk chocolate just yet.

STEP 2

While the chocolate is melting, cover a tray with baking paper and lay the popcorn out flat onto the tray, making sure you don't leave any spaces.

STEP 3

Sprinkle the cashews and marshmallows over the popcorn, and then pour the melted chocolate over the top of everything, covering as much of the mixture as you can. Place in the fridge.

STEP 4

After two hours in the fridge, the chocolate will be holding everything together. Use a knife to smash the mixture into chunks, and get ready to have your mind blown!

NEXT LEVEL
If you're feeling game, try caramelising your own popcorn by mixing together some homemade caramel and coating the popcorn with it before laying it on the tray.

TIP
Party popcorn is best consumed with friends, so be sure to invite your pals over for munchies and a movie night.

MAKE PEANUT-BUTTER COOKIE-DOUGH BALLS

Okay, so can we talk about peanut butter? It's gooey, it's sticky and it's just downright delicious. The only thing that comes close to competing is our love for cookie dough, so naturally, throwing them both in a bowl could only lead to one thing: awesomeness.

You will need:
- ⅓ cup butter, melted
- ⅓ cup packed brown sugar
- 1 tablespoon vanilla essence
- ⅓ cup peanut butter, melted
- 1 cup flour
- ½ cup dark chocolate chips

STEP 1

Place all the ingredients (minus the choc chips and flour) into a bowl, and beat until combined. Then add the flour, and continue to beat, finishing off by kneading with your hands for 30 seconds. Add an extra teaspoon or two of butter if your mixture is too crumbly.

STEP 2

Add the choc chips and mix them in with your hands or a spoon.

STEP 3

Roll the mixture into small balls with your hands and place them on a tray.

STEP 4

Place the tray in the fridge and let the balls set for an hour before you let loose on these babies. It may be the longest hour of your life, but we promise they taste better once they've set!

TRICK
Opt for organic peanut butter with no additives to make the balls a little healthier.

TIP
You can sub in M&Ms instead of choc chips if you're feeling festive.

NEXT LEVEL
If you really want to get your tastebuds dancing, put ice-cream in between two of these bad boys to make a sandwich (the naughty kind).

WANT MORE DOUGH?
For more ideas involving cookie dough (yum!), head to howtwolive.com/howtwoprojects.

BLEND A BERRILICIOUS SMOOTHIE

Nothing kicks off your day quite like a tall glass of ice-cold fruitiness. Not only do smoothies fit in with our desire to get things done quickly in the morning, they're also packed with all the good stuff you need to stay alive, awake, alert and enthusiastic, all day long!

You will need:
- 1 cup berries, fresh or frozen
- 1 large ripe banana
- 2 tablespoons Greek yoghurt
- ⅓ cup milk
- 1 teaspoon honey
- 3 ice cubes

STEP 1

Throw all of the ingredients (except the ice cubes) into your blender and blast away for about a minute. Use whatever berries you like – we usually opt for a mix.

STEP 2

Add ice cubes and blend for an additional 30 seconds – saving this step till the end prevents your 'smoothie' becoming a 'waterie'.

TRICK
Try making the ice cubes from coconut water instead of plain water. Mmmm … delicious *and* nutritious.

FEEL THE BENEFITS!
- strawberries: for glowing skin
- blueberries: stay healthy
- raspberries: energy booster

WHIP UP CHOC-BANANA POPS

When it comes to ice-cream, we believe only two opinions are legit: I love it, or I love it so much I want to roll around in a bathtub full of it. And do we have good news for all you ice-cream addicts! We've found a way to enjoy this magical creation while still getting a little nutrition. It seems almost too good to be true, but we can vouch for these choc-banana pops. They're easy to make (even for those of us who struggle with boiling a kettle) and taste like the real deal.

You will need:
- 6 large ripe bananas
- ⅔ cup Nutella
- ½ cup milk of your choice

STEP 1

Slice the bananas and place them in the freezer for one to two hours.

STEP 2

Put the bananas into a blender/food processor and blend until the mixture has a creamy consistency. Add the Nutella and milk, and blend for an extra minute.

STEP 3

Pour the mixture into a popsicle tray and put the tray in the freezer for an hour.

TRICK
If you don't have a good food processor, you can just freeze whole bananas on sticks, and then dip them in melted chocolate.

TIP
Swap the Nutella for other ingredients to create different flavours – think peanut butter or berries!

BONUS!

MAGICAL FOOD COMBOS YOU NEVER KNEW EXISTED

- celery + peanut butter
- chocolate milk + salt
- salt & vinegar chips + M&Ms
- dark chocolate + parmesan cheese
- cottage cheese + strawberries
- Nutella + porridge
- tuna + Pringles
- corn chips + egg salad
- avocado + choc-chip cookies
- mango + chilli powder
- sweet potato + marshmallows (baked)
- vanilla ice-cream + honey
- yoghurt + choc chips
- fetta + watermelon
- omelette + strawberry jam

HOW TWO
MAKE AN IMPACT!
WITH YOUR KITCHEN SKILLS

Get together with your friends and hold a bake sale at a school or university, then donate the funds raised to your charity of choice. You can even hand out flyers during the bake sale to raise awareness for the cause.

CREATE FLORAL CAT EARS

Flower crowns are sooo last season, so we've decided to give our old buddy the flick in favour of her younger, quirkier sister. Adding floral cat ears to an outfit will give you an instant meow factor that will leave festival eyes wandering from the stage.

You will need:
- 2 × 30cm pieces of wire
- an old plain headband
- a hot-glue gun
- fake flowers

STEP 1

Take one of the pieces of wire and bend it in the middle to form a triangle shape. Make sure you keep the point of the triangle a little rounded, as this will be the tip of the cat ear.

STEP 2

Hold the bottom of the triangle against the headband where you want the ear to sit, and then wrap both ends of the wire around the headband. If the ear's a little wobbly, use some glue to keep it in place. Repeat with the other ear.

STEP 3

Now it's time to add the finishing touch. Using the hot-glue gun, put glue onto each flower and then stick them onto the wire one by one. Repeat until the wire is entirely covered but there's a hole in the middle of the ear.

TIP
If you're ready to kiss your flower crown goodbye for good, use the flowers from this instead of buying new ones.

TRICK
For a bolder statement you can supersize your ears by using longer pieces of wire.

To hide the wire, wrap and glue petals around it before you start sticking the flowers down.

NEXT LEVEL
Spray the flowers with a light layer of glitter before you get gluing for some extra sparkle.

DESIGN YOUR OWN
GLITTER TATTOO

In case you didn't get the bright shiny memo, we love all things sparkly and colourful – anything that combines these two qualities is more than alright by us. These tattoos are a perfect example, and they're always at the top of our checklist when getting ready pre-festival.

You will need:
- marker/texta
- clear contact (like you use to cover your books)
- scissors
- 2 paintbrushes
- eyelash glue
- fine glitter

STEP 1

Draw the shape of your tattoo onto the paper side of the contact and cut the shape out, making sure you're careful with the scissors as you'll be using the outer area as a stencil. You can throw away the middle cut-out bit. We suggest starting with something simple like a love heart or lightning bolt.

STEP 2

Once you've decided where you'd like the tattoo, take the paper backing off and stick the contact directly onto your skin. Then, using one of the paintbrushes, fill in your tattoo shape with the eyelash glue.

STEP 3

Use the other brush to fill the tattoo with glitter. Don't be afraid to pile it on: you want the whole area to be covered!

TRICK
If drawing isn't your thing, you can trace the outline from a picture.

TIP
Use your fingers to apply the glitter if you find the paintbrush a little difficult to use.

WE LOVE
Matching tattoos! All of your friends can have the same tattoo, but each one in their fave colour.

STEP 4
Brush away any excess glitter around the tattoo, and remove the contact from your arm to reveal a sparkly masterpiece that will definitely last your crazy day of dancing.

NEXT LEVEL
Use a bunch of different glitter colours to create a rainbow tattoo.

GLITTER BOMB
If you love glitter tattoos, head to howtwolive. com/howtwoprojects for more ideas.

STYLE A FLAWLESS FESTIVAL OUTFIT

Spending time styling a killer outfit before a festival can get a little stressful, but we've got the perfect method to get you in your gear and ready to rock. Stick with us and pretty soon you'll be worrying less about putting together your own get-up – which means more time to spy on the crazy cool outfits everyone else is wearing!

LOOK 1

If you're the type of gal who'll be hitting the d-floor hard all day, this one's for you. Denim cut-offs and a singlet are festival staples, so why not jazz things up with a fun vest and tassel bag?

LOOK 2

Music, what music? To you festivals are all about getting dressed up and having fun with your friends. A long skirt and bowler hat will give off the perfect laid-back vibe, while still allowing you to squeeze in a little dance.

LOOK 3

Whether you're a real rock chick or you just like to play one, an oversized singlet and lace flares are your festie bestie. Take your outfit to the next level with a backpack and biker boots that'll keep you banging to the beat all night long.

LOOK 1

LOOK 2

LOOK 3

DON'T FORGET
Nobody likes squinting in photos, so make sure you bring your fave sunnies!

TIP
Always opt for a comfy pair of shoes. Blisters are not your friend.

WE LOVE
Stacking lots of bracelets and rings when going to a festival – this is the best time to get away with being OTT.

PUT TOGETHER YOUR
PRE-FESTIVAL PLAYLIST

There's no denying that seeing an artist live is much more fun when you've jammed along to their songs once or twice before, so as soon as the festival line-up is released, it's time to get your playlist going.

STEP 1

After you've sussed out which of your favourite artists are going to be playing, have a look through the program for some cool acts whose songs you don't really know.

STEP 2

Download a few songs from each of your chosen artists – the ones you love as well as your soon-to-be faves. Make sure you're jumping on their biggest and latest tracks, as these are the ones that will most likely be played. Also check out websites like setlist.fm to find out what other songs bands have played at recent concerts.

STEP 3

Put together a few different playlists, sorted into your various music personalities – party, chill out, scream at the top of your lungs, etc – then listen to nothing else for the week preceding the festival to get you totally in the zone!

TRICK
Not going to have any power at the festival? You can make music speakers using two plastic cups and a toilet-paper roll. Make a hole in the side of each cup and push the ends of the toilet roll through each hole. Then make a hole in the top of the toilet roll for your phone to sit in.

TIP
Make sure you've got your killer pair of headphones ready so you can listen on the go.

BONUS!

FESTIVAL PACKING CHECKLIST

The Essentials:
- [ ] your fave sunnies
- [ ] shoulder bag
- [ ] sun hat
- [ ] earplugs
- [ ] eye mask
- [ ] cute water bottle
- [ ] portable phone charger
- [ ] torch
- [ ] first-aid kit (think bandaids, scissors, headache tablets)

The Cosmetics Kit:
- [ ] bronzer
- [ ] mascara
- [ ] waterproof sunscreen
- [ ] lip balm
- [ ] hairbrush
- [ ] dry shampoo
- [ ] face wipes
- [ ] compact mirror
- [ ] nail file

The Fun Stuff:
- [ ] bindis and body jewels
- [ ] music speakers
- [ ] costumes
- [ ] water guns
- [ ] face paint
- [ ] playing cards
- [ ] hula hoops
- [ ] bubble blower
- [ ] picnic rug

MAKE AN IMPACT!

BY SHARING THE FESTIVAL LOVE

Music is one of the best ways to lift a mood, so if someone you know needs cheering up, offer to take them to a concert or festival. If you have time beforehand, bake a few goodies to be shared during the event.

KEEP YOUR HAIR HEALTHY

We often get asked, 'How do you grow your hair so long?' After chanting 'Rapunzel' ten times while standing on one leg didn't help, we discovered this incredible eggocado mask. It's super easy to make and helps to moisturise, strengthen and grow your hair. Sound good? Our hair seems to think so, and if you get a little bored while waiting, make sure you have some corn chips on hand to go with your hair dip … (it's probably a better idea to make a little extra dip for eating purposes).

You will need:
- 1 egg yolk
- half an avocado, mashed

STEP 1

Whisk the egg yolk in a bowl, then mix in the avocado. Keep the mixture a little lumpy.

STEP 2

Wet your hair and apply the mask, starting with your scalp and moving towards the ends. Massage the mask into your scalp for five minutes.

STEP 3

Wash the mask out with cold water, rinsing thoroughly until it's all gone. Afterwards, shampoo and condition as usual, and enjoy your newly luscious locks!

WE LOVE
Using this mask once a month to keep our hair game strong.

TIP
If you have long hair, double the recipe so you have enough to cover your ends.

NEXT LEVEL
Try adding some sour cream to the mixture for extra shine.

MAINTAIN YOUR BROWS

We have to admit we were a little hesitant when bushy brows came back in style, but once Cara Delevingne showed us how it's done, we came around pretty quickly. These days, doing your eyebrows before you leave the house trumps mascara, lip gloss and pretty much any other beauty routine, so get ready to prep your brows to perfection.

STEP 1

Use tweezers to pluck stray hairs once a fortnight. This will ensure your eyebrows are always looking manicured, and cut down on visits to the brow bar – bonus!

STEP 2

If you want to give your brows a bit of a boost, try rubbing argan oil into them every night before you go to bed. This will promote growth and thickness (but don't worry, it won't encourage old man bushiness!).

STEP 3

If you have brows like ours that are a little unruly, we recommend applying some hair gel to them using an eyebrow brush. This will help your eyebrows stay in place and also give great definition.

NEXT LEVEL

Get bolder brows with the subtle use of an eyebrow wand. For best results choose a colour that's one shade lighter than your brows.

STYLE-OFF: EYEBROW PENCIL VS EYEBROW WAND

The verdict: eyebrow wand wins! Combing through your brows with a wand is no muss, no fuss, which is just what we want when getting our face on in the morning. Wands also help your brows look bold but still natural. If you haven't completely mastered the pencil, you risk ending up with the nickname Gracie Lou Freebush.

GET GLOWING SKIN

Getting a facial sounds like a great idea in theory, but the reality – having your face pricked, prodded and squeezed – will likely leave you bashing your heels together wishing you were back in Kansas. This at-home face mask recipe is soothing for your skin and can be made with ingredients you'll probably have lying around your kitchen. Move over movie night: it's time to get the girls around for an evening of manis and masks.

You will need:
- ½ ripe banana
- 2 tablespoons honey
- 1 tablespoon cinnamon

STEP 1

Use a fork to mash up the banana, and then mix in the honey and cinnamon. Don't stress if your mixture is a little lumpy.

STEP 2

Cleanse your face so it's completely clean, then apply the mask all over your face and neck.

STEP 3

Let the mask sit for approximately 10 minutes. Now would be a great time to give yourself a quickie mani.

STEP 4

Wash the mask off with warm water and a face washer. Don't forget to apply a moisturiser with SPF before heading out to flaunt your new radiant skin.

TIP
Try using the same mask on your hands and feet to keep them feeling soft.

WE LOVE
Snapping silly pics in our banana masks (but we're careful not to accidentally post them on Instagram!).

GOOD FACE
For more fun face masks, head to howtwolive.com/howtwoprojects!

MIX UP A REFRESHING BODY SCRUB

Khaleesi may love her dragons, but that doesn't mean she wants to have scaly skin of her own! We can only assume to get her silky smooth bod, Khaleesi uses a scrub like this one: it's full of sugar, spice and all things nice, and will keep your skin radiant all year long.

You will need:
- ⅓ cup granulated sugar
- 2 tablespoons olive oil
- loofah (optional)

STEP 1

Combine the sugar with the oil and mix well.

STEP 2

Using your hands or a loofah, rub the scrub into your skin wherever you feel like you need it, paying special attention to naturally dry areas like elbows and knees.

STEP 3

Wash the scrub off in the shower.

SILKY SMOOTH SCRUB

NEXT LEVEL
Try adding these essential oils for added benefits (just a few drops will do):

- carrot seed oil – reduces the appearance of scars
- lavender oil – helps you relax
- jasmine oil – gives an extra burst of moisture

BONUS!

BEAUTY TRICKS & TIPS

- If you run out of shaving cream, use hair conditioner instead
- Moisturise your hair by putting beer in it and leaving for a few minutes
- Soak your freshly painted fingernails in cold water for three minutes to help them dry faster
- Squeeze lemon juice onto your hair while you're in the sun to lighten it
- Place damp chamomile tea bags under your eyes to reduce puffiness
- Make a mixture of baking soda and water to fix fake-tan mishaps
- Use baby powder or flour if you've run out of dry shampoo
- Use honey as a substitute for lip balm

- Soak your feet in milk and water to keep them soft
- Dry your hair with a cotton t-shirt instead of a towel to prevent frizzy hair
- Moisturise your body with olive oil or coconut oil
- Dab flaxseed oil along your lash line to help your lashes grow

HOW TWO
MAKE AN IMPACT!

WHEN IT'S PAMPER TIME

Invite the girls over for a spa day, and ask them to bring a $5 donation for entry. Play a game while you're waiting for masks to dry and have the winner choose which charity the collected money will go towards.

MASTER THE PARTY LIP

If you're a nude eyes/bold lips kinda gal, then oh boy are you going to go gaga for this one. It's time to push plain old coloured lips aside, whip out the glitter and add a touch of disco to your pout.

You will need:
- lip balm
- lipstick
- lip gloss
- paintbrush/lip brush
- glitter

STEP 1

Time to prep your lips. Begin by applying lip balm, followed by a thin layer of your go-to shade of lippie. Top this off with some shiny lip gloss and then you're ready to get glittering.

STEP 2

Using a paintbrush or lip brush, dab loose glitter all over your lips. You can use glitter from a craft store, or track down some cosmetic glitter.

TIP
Make sure the colour of the glitter matches your lipstick/lip gloss shade.

DON'T FORGET
Take a little extra glitter and a brush in your purse for touch-ups later.

WE LOVE
Making our sparkly lips the focus by keeping eye make-up to a minimum.

PUT ON COLOURED LASHES

Have you ever heard someone say, 'I wish I wore more black'? Didn't think so. Add an extra pop of colour to your outfit by swapping black lashes for something with a little more sass. It's a serious mood-lifter and all the cool kids are doing it (think Katy Perry and Lady Gaga!).

You will need:
- coloured false eyelashes
- tweezers
- eyelash glue

STEP 1

Choose your lashes – this can be tricky as they come in all shapes and sizes. If you're a falsie first-timer, we suggest going for a basic shape in your fave hue as they take a little while to get used to. You'll find the best selection of fake lashes on eBay.

STEP 2

Hold the lashes with tweezers and slowly apply eyelash glue along their base. Then place the falsies along your natural lash line, pressing your eyelashes and the false ones between your fingers to help everything set.

WARNING
Until you're used to them, wearing false lashes feels a little like you've got butterflies sitting on your eyelids.

TIP
Use an eyelash curler and mascara before you apply your falsies for some extra oomph.

TRICK
Opt for white glue instead of dark as it dries clear so you won't see the excess glue.

WE LOVE
Matching our lash colour to our eye colour – this really make your eyes pop.

ROCK A FISHTAIL BRAID

We have to admit the fishtail braid is something that's taken us a while to master, but it's one of those things that suddenly clicks and then you never forget it – kind of like riding a dolphin. Follow these easy steps and you'll be braiding with the best of them in no time.

STEP 1

Begin by tying your hair in a low ponytail, then split your hair in two.

STEP 2

Using your finger, separate a small piece of your hair from the outer edge of the left bunch, and cross it over, adding it to the inner side of the right bunch.

STEP 3

Repeat this all the way down your ponytail, alternating sides each time. Make sure the pieces you use are roughly the same size so your braid stays neat.

STEP 4

To finish, tie your braid with an elastic, and then cut the elastic at the top of your hair off.

TRICK
For a more effortless look, loosen your braid a little after you've finished it.

TIP
Try practising on a friend before tackling your own hair.

WE LOVE
Pairing a fishtail braid with a flowing dress and sandals for an easy summer look.

APPLY HAIR CHALK

Okay, we admit it: we're huge hair-commitment phobes. Mention cutting, dyeing or anything else that requires us to commit for more than a week, and we're outta there faster than you can say Gretchen Wieners. So when we found out about hair chalk, it felt like we'd just been told it was socially acceptable to lick the icing off the cupcake and then move onto the next one.

STEP 1

First you'll need to get your paws on some hair chalk. You can find it at most big pharmacies for as little as $5.

STEP 2

Wet the section of your hair where you want to apply the chalk. If you're blonde, apply it to dry hair, unless you want the chalk to stay on longer.

STEP 3

Next, apply the chalk in a downward motion, twisting the hair as you draw, as this friction will allow the chalk to release more colour.

STEP 4

After it has dried, use a straightening iron on your hair to set the colour. Finish with hairspray.

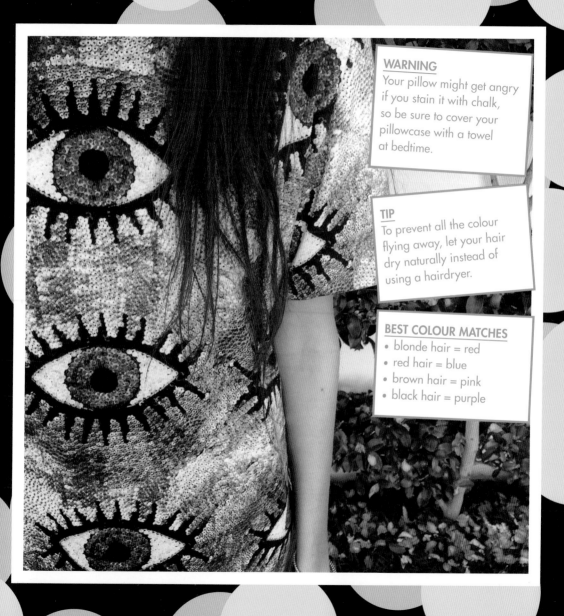

WARNING
Your pillow might get angry if you stain it with chalk, so be sure to cover your pillowcase with a towel at bedtime.

TIP
To prevent all the colour flying away, let your hair dry naturally instead of using a hairdryer.

BEST COLOUR MATCHES
- blonde hair = red
- red hair = blue
- brown hair = pink
- black hair = purple

BONUS!

MAKE-UP DOS & DON'TS

- Do line the inside of your eyes with white eyeliner to make your eyes look bigger
- Don't overload on lip gloss
- Do apply eyeliner to your top eyelids for an evening out
- Don't line your lips with a different colour to your lipstick
- Do use a light concealer under your eyes
- Don't forget to clean nail polish off the edges of your nails
- Do create more dramatic eyebrows using an eyebrow wand
- Don't get overexcited with the bronzer
- Do add a hint of blush to your nose for a sun-kissed look
- Don't forget to blend your neck when applying foundation

- Do apply a serum before using anything heated on your hair
- Don't hold your hot curler or straightener on your hair in one place for too long
- Do opt for a messy updo when your hair needs a wash
- Don't go overboard on the hairspray
- Do use a hair straightener to create soft waves

MAKE AN IMPACT!

AS A HAIR & MAKE-UP PRO

Volunteer to do hair and make-up at a local school fete or play. Everything's more fun with a friend, so get a pal involved and you'll be able to offer twice the help.

CREATE CONFETTI NAILS

Confetti nails are a great place for beginners to start, as all that's required is for you to be the queen of the dotting tool (which is easy), and for you to have fun (which is, well, fun!). These nails are pretty festive so we recommend wearing them to a surprise party. Surprise, confetti nails!

You will need:
- white nail polish, plus as many nail polish colours as you like for the confetti
- a dotting tool or bobby pin

STEP 1

Paint all of your nails white.

STEP 2

Use the dotting tool to dot on one colour. The aim is to have a big cluster of confetti at the nail tip, and gradually less as you go towards your cuticle, so dot more near the top.

STEP 3

Once the first colour has dried, continue to add colours, one at a time. Add as many or as few as you like until you're happy with the result (we tend to go confetti crazy but you might prefer something simpler).

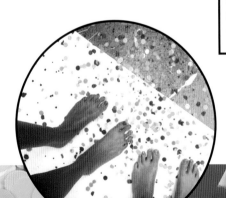

TIP
Lightly dot the confetti spots on, stopping just before the dotting tool hits your nail.

NEXT LEVEL
To brighten things up even more, use a colour as the base instead of white.

STYLE-OFF: BRIGHT CONFETTI VS PASTEL CONFETTI
The verdict: pastel confetti wins! Pastel colours tend to complement each other more than the brights, so with all these colours in the one little place, our top pick goes to the pastels.

GET RAINBOW NAILS

They say less is more, but whoever 'they' are must be having a pretty boring time while we're over here having ourselves a nail-art party! If your nails are still living in the noughties, it's time to wipe off your French manicure and get on board with nails done the HTL way – with rainbows.

You will need:
- a sponge
- nail polish (four colours)
- a bobby pin or dotting tool

TIP
Mix two nail polish colours together on a piece of foil to create a colour you don't have.

WE LOVE
Choosing colours that blend into each other, for example, yellow to orange to pink to red.

NEXT LEVEL
Paint your nails white before you sponge on the rainbow to make the colours really pop.

STEP 1

Take the sponge and put four thick stripes of nail polish on it, one in each colour. Make sure the length of the total area you've painted on matches the length of your nails. Blend the colours together slightly using a bobby pin or dotting tool.

STEP 2

Sponge the colours onto your nail in one motion. You can dab the nail with the sponge in the same spot a few times in order to make the rainbow brighter. Repeat this process for each nail. Be sure to clean around your nails with a cotton bud and some nail polish remover!

DESIGN CUPCAKE NAILS

The only place we like cupcakes more than in our stomachs is on our nails. These are a great choice if you're looking for minimal effort but maximum effect … and just think how cute you'll look turning up to afternoon tea with these party treats on your fingertips!

You will need:
- pink, white and red nail polish
- a dotting tool or bobby pin
- a few extra nail polishes (for sprinkles, we like blue, yellow, purple)

STEP 1

Paint all your nails with the pink polish.

STEP 2

Using the dotting tool, dot on the white icing, starting with the tip of your nail and coming a third of the way down, leaving the bottom two-thirds plain pink.

STEP 3

Once the icing has dried, add a dot of red to the top of the icing to look like a cherry.

STEP 4

Use as many colours as you like to dot on little sprinkles to the icing.

WARNING

Once you master these babies, your friends will be lining up for you to paint *their* nails.

TIP

Have the girls over for an afternoon of cupcake baking and cupcake nail painting!

NEXT LEVEL

Instead of using pink for the base of your cupcake, choose five different colours so each nail is a different coloured cupcake.

PAINT WATERMELON NAILS

Okay girl, enough with the junk food: it's time to put those nails on a diet. Ten cuticle push-ups and a few juicy slices of watermelon ought to do it. And don't let us catch you making eyes at any more of those cupcakes (see p. 80)!

You will need:
- pink, white, green and black nail polish
- a dotting tool, bobby pin or detailing brush

STEP 1

Paint all your nails with the pink nail polish.

STEP 2

Use the white polish to create a tip, like you would for a French manicure.

STEP 3

Once the white has dried, do the same thing with the green, but finish slightly higher up on your nail so you can still see a bit of the white.

STEP 4

Now it's time to add the seeds using the dotting tool or detailing brush. Seedless watermelons might be all the rage right now, but trust us: this step is the key to getting your nails looking fruitilicious.

TIP
Once you've mastered the watermelon, why not incorporate some other fruits and make your fingertips a fruit salad?

WE LOVE
Changing it up and painting yellow melons instead of pink ones.

NEXT LEVEL
Add some glitter over the top of your watermelons.

MAKE FRIENDS WITH SALAD
Head to howtwolive.com/howtwoprojects for more fruity nail tutorials.

BONUS!

NAIL ART KIT

It's easy to buy your nail art tools online, but if you're just looking to have a little fun with the girls at home, we've included some quick substitutes that will also do the trick.

Nail Polishes
Make sure you have black, white and a selection of your fave colours.

Cosmetics Case
Mozi and Wicked Sista are two of our favourite brands for cute cases.

Manicure Strips
Swap manicure strips for masking tape.

A Detailing Brush
Swap a detailing brush for any paintbrush; just cut the bristles until the brush is thin enough (around a quarter of the size of a standard nail polish brush).

Sponges
Swap a fancy nail sponge for your kitchen sponge (just don't use it to clean the dishes later!).

Nail Pens
Instead of a black nail pen, use a thin permanent marker. These are great for outlining and are way easier to use than the real thing!

Dotting Tools
Swap a dotting tool for the tip of a bobby pin.

HOW TWO
MAKE AN IMPACT!
WITH YOUR KNACK FOR NAIL ART

Now that you're a nail-art pro, offer to visit a local hospital and paint children's nails. You'll cheer the kids up with a chat, and their colourful nails will leave them smiling all week long.

BLOGGING

SHARE YOUR BLOG PROGRESS WITH US:

#howtwolive #howtwoblog

COME UP WITH A CONCEPT

STEP 1

Clear your schedule for the arvo, and write a list of your likes and dislikes. It's important to start with your own ideas, before you go off and seek influence from other sources.

STEP 2

Think about your talents and expertise, and try to come up with ways you could apply these to your concept. Incorporating a special skill shows you have a unique perspective and could be the key to making your blog stand out from all the rest.

Starting a blog without a concept is like ordering gelato without asking for two or three tasters first – you've gotta take some time to come up with the perfect combo, and then you'll be ready to dig in! We've come up with a few steps to help get your creative juices flowing.

STEP 3

Get Googling! Look at a range of different blogs and websites for inspo and write down the qualities that you do and don't like. You want your blog to be completely unique, so make sure you look at as many different kinds of sites as possible. Sign up to a website like stumbleupon.com, which suggests websites you might like based on your interests.

STEP 4

Lay out all the lists you've created, and think about how you can bring your various ideas together into one killer concept. Think through a bunch of different concepts before deciding which one will work best.

TIP

Be original. If you want to focus on something like fashion news, put your own spin on it, the way Perez Hilton burst onto the scene with his funny doodles and outlandish comments.

DON'T FORGET

Once you've come up with a concept, stick to it! Rolling with one idea and being persistent will always be better than starting from scratch over and over again.

NEXT LEVEL

Present your three favourite blog concepts to your friends, and have them vote to decide which one you should go with. If your friends like it, chances are others will too!

SET UP YOUR BLOG

STEP 1

First you need to decide which blogging platform you want to go with.

- Blogger is the easiest to use and is owned by Google, so if you have an existing Gmail account you can use this to log in.
- WordPress is the most customisable. If you're going to get a web designer to put your blog together, this will be your best bet.
- Tumblr is good if you prefer to say it with photos. This is a cross between a blogging platform and a social media site, so people will be able to share your pics super easily.

Bringing your blog to life only takes a few clicks, but you'll feel like you've accomplished a heap and be well on your way to blogging superstardom!

STEP 2

Now it's time to bring the page to life. You can download free themes, which control the look of your blog, from tons of websites, or you can head to somewhere like themeforest.net, where you can buy themes for as little as a few dollars. The theme you apply will change things like headings, fonts and layout, so make sure you choose one that suits the style of your blog, as keeping things consistent is the best way to build a strong brand.

STEP 3

Once your blog is full of personality from the theme you've chosen, you'll be ready to start posting. Make sure you post regularly to help build up your audience, and don't forget to share your posts on social media.

TIP
Take a look at blogs on all the different platforms, and work out which you like the look of most.

Visit youtube.com/howtwolive where you'll find videos with further tips on blogging.

TRICK
Commenting on other blogs and including a link to your own is a great way to bring traffic to your blog.

NEXT LEVEL
Buy the domain name with your blog's title (eg howtwolive.com) and redirect the page to your blog. You can do this easily using a website like godaddy.com. This will help you look more professional while allowing you to remain on your platform of choice.

TAKE A GOOD OUTFIT SHOT

STEP 1

Hit the streets with your camera in one hand and your bestie in the other. Wide streets or parks are often the best for shooting. Be sure to avoid anywhere that's too busy, as you don't want people getting in the way of your epic shot.

STEP 2

Take turns swapping between being the photographer and the subject so you can both learn the ropes. The photographer should stand far enough away from the subject to get the full outfit in, bending down a little in order to make the subject appear taller.

While we all wish we lived in the beautiful streets of Paris, where taking the perfect outfit photo is as simple as stepping out your front door, this is unfortunately not the case for most of us. We work our booties off trying to take the perfect snap, and getting a few pro tips along the way can never hurt.

STEP 3

Snap as many pics as possible so you can go back later and analyse what worked and what didn't. Professionals never get the job done in one shot; the more options you have, the more likely you are to have that one winner.

TIP
Shoot early morning or late afternoon, as these times have the best light. Overcast days also provide better shooting conditions, as you're less likely to end up with harsh shadows.

TRICK
Try having the photographer stand a little further back and use the zoom. This is how bloggers create the sharp subject/blurred background effect.

NEXT LEVEL
If you want to kick your photography skills up a notch, try an online photography course – finding one that suits is easy with a course directory website like skilledup.com.

RECORD A KICK-ASS VIDEO

STEP 1

Come up with an idea for your video. It can be really helpful to see what else has been going viral lately, so start by checking out what websites like buzzfeed.com and elitedaily.com have been featuring.

STEP 2

Now it's time to get shooting. Keep in mind that practice makes perfect, so if it's your first time getting serious in front of the camera, watch each take back so you can see what you did well and what needs changing up.

While it can be hard to compete with a cat playing a keyboard or an adorable baby biting his brother's finger, we promise getting your video seen by thousands is easier than you think, and we've got a few simple steps to help you go viral.

STEP 3

Don't forget to edit your video. These days, computers usually come with free video-editing software, like iMovie for Macs, which are pretty user-friendly.

STEP 4

Where you post the video will have a huge impact on how popular it gets, so post it in as many places as possible, including YouTube, Vimeo and Facebook. To get the word out even further, ask your friends to share it on all their social media sites too.

TIP
Videos that go viral are usually between 30 and 90 seconds long, so be sure to get to the point quickly.

TRICK
If you've never edited videos before, watch a couple of quick YouTube tutorials to get started.

DON'T FORGET
It's more about the content quality than the camera quality, so don't stress if all you have is an iPhone.

WE LOVE
Videos that make us laugh or cry, or teach us something new.

QUIZ: WHAT'S YOUR BLOG CALLING?

1. What do you spend most of your time on?
a) Instagram
b) YouTube
c) Tumblr

2. What was your favourite subject at school?
a) English
b) Drama
c) Art

3. What do your friends rely on you for?
a) Fashion tips
b) Laughter
c) Advice

4. What would you use a camera for?
a) Taking bad-ass selfies
b) Recording an epic video
c) Snapping up a storm

5. Who is your favourite celebrity?
a) Emma Stone
b) Miley Cyrus
c) Taylor Swift

Mostly As: Personal Style File
Sounds like you'd be perfect for a personal style blog. Share photos of your outfits, offer style advice, and invite your followers on your fashionable journey.

Mostly Bs: Viral Vlogger
Videos are a super fun way to interact with your followers. Start a website or video channel where people can tune in for your latest updates.

Mostly Cs: Inspiration Nation
Why not start a blog where you can share your inspiration with your followers? Think photos, cool quotes, patterns and whatever else reflects your personal taste.

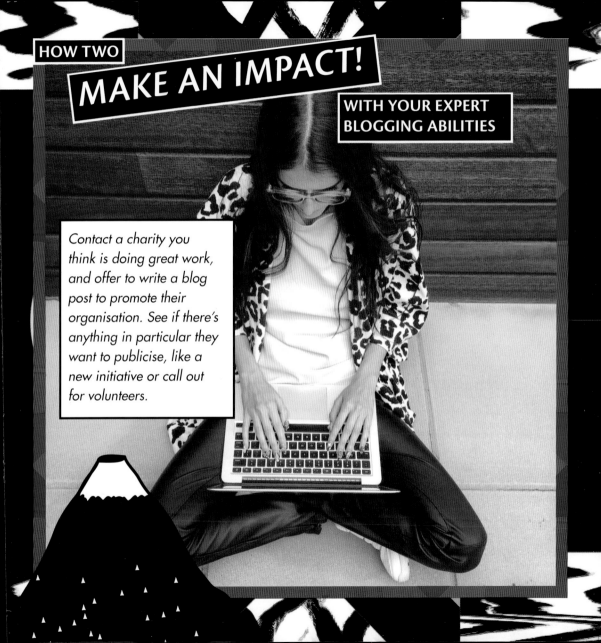

HOW TWO
MAKE AN IMPACT!
WITH YOUR EXPERT BLOGGING ABILITIES

Contact a charity you think is doing great work, and offer to write a blog post to promote their organisation. See if there's anything in particular they want to publicise, like a new initiative or call out for volunteers.

BUILD YOUR SOCIAL
MEDIA FOLLOWING

Computer nerds are a thing of the past – these days if you know how the internet works, you probably have more cyber friends than Taylor Swift has cats. If you're struggling to keep up with the new popular, fear not: we've got some top tips to help build your followers.

STEP 1

Consistency is key: you need to be uploading regularly to get noticed. Aim to post a few times throughout the day, but if that's not possible we recommend you try for at least three to four times a week to see results.

STEP 2

Interacting with other people online is a great way to get your name out there, so comment, like, re-tweet and favourite as much as you can.

STEP 3

When you wear different brands, tag and @ them in your posts. If a brand likes your photos, they might repost one and your followers will instantly increase. Jackpot!

STEP 4

Team up with people your followers might be interested in hearing about (eg a fellow foodie or someone with similar style to you), and 'share for share' – agree to post about each other. This way you'll both likely see an increase in your following.

TIP
Post on your most popular channel about your other social media accounts to get the word out.

NEXT LEVEL
If you're trying to grow as a blogger or business, team up with a brand to run a giveaway, and make sure they'll post about it so you'll get their followers and vice versa.

MASTER THE SELFIE

While anyone can point and click a camera at themselves, these days the word 'selfie' means a whole lot more than that. Perfect lighting and flattering angles are just two of many things to consider if you want to keep up with the trend flooding social media. The secret to the perfect selfie is knowing what works best for your features, so grab a mirror and get familiar with that babe staring back at you.

STEP 1

Find a light source – this can be a lamp, window or sunshine – and face towards it.

STEP 2

Flip your camera so you can see yourself on the screen, and holding the phone in your dominant hand, stretch your arm out until your whole face is visible on screen.

STEP 3

Use the screen to play with different angles and decide what works best for your face. If you feel a little awkward, just think how much time Kylie Jenner must spend doing this!

STEP 4

Click away! Snap lots of different expressions and angles, and afterwards you can look back and decide what worked and what didn't.

WARNING
Make sure you're aware of what's behind you – coloured walls and patterned wallpaper are great, but you don't want to accidentally expose your messy bedroom!

DON'T FORGET
Holding the camera below eye level can create a double chin – great for pulling silly faces, but otherwise best to avoid.

TIP
Selfie sticks are fun to use with your friends, but can often produce unflattering pics. If you're rocking the solo selfie, we suggest keeping it old school and opting for your arm instead.

TAKE THE PERFECT FLAT LAY

Now you may be thinking that flat laying is for fashion bloggers only, but we're about to show you that mastering this art is as simple as baking a cake … from a packet, of course. Practice makes perfect, so make sure you give this one a few goes, and your social media cred will increase as quickly as your followers.

You will need:
- items to arrange (eg clothes, flowers, accessories)
- your phone or a camera

STEP 1

Choose your subjects wisely. We suggest selecting one really cool piece to start with, and use this to guide the other objects you pick, thinking about shapes, sizes and colours. Try sticking to one or two different colours, as flat lays look best when colours are kept consistent.

STEP 2

Place your main piece in either a corner or the centre of your flat lay, then arrange the other items around it. The flat lay should be in the shape of a square or rectangle (depending on what it's going to be used for), so keep that in mind when introducing new items.

STEP 3

Start shooting! A bird's eye view is always best, so snap from above. Your phone camera will be fine to start with, but if you're looking to achieve flat lay queen status, try using an SLR camera instead.

STEP 4

Once you've taken a few pics, look over them and decide whether items need to be moved slightly. Keep shooting until you're happy with the results.

TIP
You want your flat lay to be a neat mess, so avoid piling items on top of each other, but feel free to place things in different directions and play with objects of all sizes.

NEXT LEVEL
Experiment with different backgrounds – think coloured paper, printed carpets and textured floors.

EDIT YOUR PHOTOS

So you don't got mad photography skills but you still want to upload killer pics? Fortunately for you we share the same lack of talent in this department, so we've come up with some tricks to help us all look like pros: 'fake it till you make it' is about to become your personal catchphrase. Follow us friends, and we'll have your pics looking like postcards in no time.

Photo-editing apps are a serious game changer and there are a million free ones in the app store just waiting for you to download them. The best thing about all the zero-dollar price tags is that you can download a few and see which one suits you best. A couple of our faves are VSCO Cam and Adobe Photoshop Express.

Opening up a new editing program can be a little scary at first; you might feel like you're speaking English in a world full of French people. But just remember, you're here strictly on business and the best starting place is getting your head around the following four functions:

- Brightness: makes your pic lighter or darker
- Contrast: adjusts how bold your pic is
- Saturation: makes the colours more or less vibrant
- Sharpness: adjusts the definition of your pic

TIP
Saturation is great for making your skin look a little sun-kissed, but be careful not to go overboard or you'll risk looking like an oompa loompa.

TRICK
Use the crop function if anything unwanted makes it into the background of your pic.

WE LOVE
Increasing all four elements for a brighter, more vibrant photo.

BONUS!

Write to us on Twitter @howtwolive_. You'll be sure to get a response from us!

TIPS FOR GETTING A CELEB TO NOTICE YOU ON SOCIAL MEDIA

- Do the obvious, like re-tweet and comment on their posts regularly.
- Interact with them at times no-one else would (eg not while their show is playing on TV).
- Be unique and original with your posts – stay away from the standard 'please follow me' or 'I'm your biggest fan'.
- Know what you're trying to achieve and base your interactions with them around that (eg getting a job or tickets to a sold-out show).
- Find out if the celeb regularly responds to certain comments/tweets (eg people's birthdays or inspired fans).
- @ them at the beginning of the post rather than the end, to make sure they know you're speaking to them.
- Remember this is meant to be a bit of fun – make sure you're reaching out to them, not invading their privacy!

HOW TWO LIVE
SCRAPBOOK

HOW TWO LIVE'S FAVE
ONLINE STORES

ASOS Marketplace: marketplace.asos.com
If you're looking to find the next sass & bide then this is where you need to be, as hundreds of up-and-coming designers from around the world feature their epic wares.

Pixie Market: pixiemarket.com
This shop houses an eclectic combination of one-off gems and lesser-known boutique labels that are about to become your new faves.

Nasty Gal: nastygal.com
What started out as an eBay account selling vintage pieces has grown into one of the biggest and coolest online stores in the world. This is our go-to site for wardrobe staples and killer accessories.

Shop Jeen: shopjeen.com
If 'the crazier, the better' is your motto, then welcome home. There is much joy and happiness to be found scrolling through Shop Jeen's never-ending pages of next-level clothing and accessories.

O Mighty: o-mighty.com
This website could just as easily have been called O Quirky. You'll find brights and prints aplenty to pare back with your basics.

Solestruck: solestruck.com
This place might not have started our love affair with shoes, but it sure as shells has kept it alive and well for the past five years. If you're not yet a shoe addict, beware of what lies ahead.

The Grand Social: thegrandsocial.com.au
Supporting our fellow Aussies and discovering new designers are always top of our checklist when we're out shopping. This store combines both these things into one magical fashion hub that you *need* in your favourites bar.

Style Nanda: stylenanda.com
This Korean-based store is full of the cutest-patootest pieces on the internet, from oversized jersey tees to floral circle skirts. Keep in mind its sizes often run small.

Twoobs: twoobs.com
We heard these two sisters started a line of shoes that come packaged in tubes and they're all kinds of awesome … Okay, so we may be a little biased here as this is our shoe label, but we promise one click and you'll be hooked.

Stylerunner: stylerunner.com
Whether you're heading to the gym for a workout or you're a brunch-in-exercise-gear sorta gal, this store has you covered and will keep you looking stylish in the process.

CUT-OUTS

ZOMG

ABOUT THE AUTHORS

How Two Live was started by sisters Jess and Stef Dadon in 2012 as a way to keep in contact when Stef moved to Paris for six months. A cross between a daily diary and a platform for sharing their outfits, the girls document their daily lives, travels and adventures, as well as their latest wardrobe additions.

They have quickly become known for their quirky style, as well as their matching outfits, and have worked with a number of renowned Australian and international labels. They're also proactive in promoting up-and-coming designers.

'Jess and Stef [of HTL] are being crowned blog royalty thanks to their mirror-image outfit posts.'
LOOK magazine, UK

THANK YOU

We'd like to thank everyone who helped with the making of this book, including: Bella and Alex for keeping us in touch with what's cool; Dassi and Kim for lending their hands; Ronen, Elliot and Carly for pretending to be photographers; our family for their never-ending support; and everyone at Hardie Grant for all their hard work in bringing this book to life.

The publisher would like to acknowledge the following individuals and organisations:

Editorial Manager
Melissa Kayser

Project Manager
Lauren Whybrow

Editor
Michelle Bennett

Design, layout and patterns
tin&ed

Typesetting
Megan Ellis

Pre-press
Splitting Image

Photography Credits
All photos © Jess and Stef Dadon, except 3 (image circle) Helena Lester-Card; 15 (style 4 pic) Clare Plueckhahn; 33 Erika Budiman; 65 (party pic) Gavriel Maynard; 95 (under Step 4) Princess Polly; 107 Erika Budiman.

Explore Australia Publishing Pty Ltd
Ground Floor, Building 1, 658 Church St, Richmond, VIC 3121

Explore Australia Publishing Pty Ltd is a division of Hardie Grant Publishing Pty Ltd

hardie grant publishing

Published by Explore Australia Publishing Pty Ltd, 2015

Form and design © Explore Australia Publishing Pty Ltd, 2015
Concept and text © Jess and Stef Dadon, 2015

A Cataloguing-in-Publication entry is available from the catalogue of the National Library of Australia at www.nla.gov.au

ISBN-13 9781741174892
10 9 8 7 6 5 4 3 2 1

Printed and bound in China by 1010 Printing International Ltd

Publisher's note: Every effort has been made to ensure that the information in this book is accurate at the time of going to press. The publisher welcomes information and suggestions for correction or improvement. Email: info@exploreaustralia.net.au

Publisher's disclaimer: The publisher cannot accept responsibility for any errors or omissions.

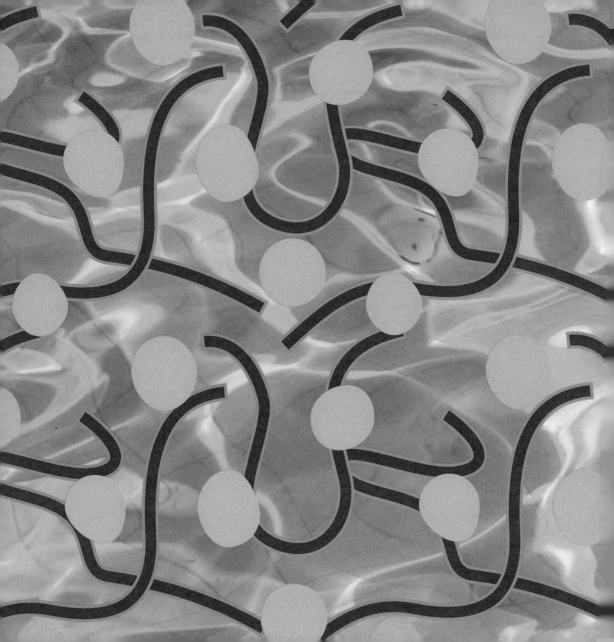